A Teaching on
Calling the Guru from Afar
devotion

◇◇◇◇◇◇◇◇

By
Dungse Lama Pema Rinpoche

Tsum Library
Tsum Monastery, Lama Gaun
Tsum-Nubri Rural Municipality
Gorkha, Nepal
www.tsummonastery.org

Translated by Khenpo David Karma Chophel.
Cover design & book layout by Acharya Ngodup Gyaltsen.
Text input by Susan Liu

Preface

These teachings were given in 2021 during the Covid pandemic. During this time, many students were isolated far from their teachers. I myself was far from His Holiness Karmapa, and far from my root guru Khenchen Thrangu Rinpoche. Many people requested me to teach something to help their devotion during this time when they were unable to see their teacher.

Although I have no good qualities myself, our wonderful translator Khenpo David Karma Choephel enabled me to pass on these teachings that I received from Khenchen Thrangu Rinpoche. We were able to accomplish this over the internet. My student Susan Liu worked tirelessly to transcribe the talks.

Our Tsum monastery then wished to publish these teachings for the benefit of students near and far. As a result of all of those good wishes, this book has come to be. Whatever mistakes are contained in it are mine alone.

Sarva Mangalam

Contents

We are pleased to publish a new book *"Devotion"* by Dungse Lama Pema Rinpoche.

During the Covid-19 pandemic, Dungse Lama Pema Rinpoche offered teachings on *"Calling the Guru from Afar"* via zoom to his dharma friends.

Dungse Rinpoche teaches with current examples, easy to understand, and he shares his own experiences, which we can relate with ourselves. Rinpoche explains that our life is so precious, why we should treasure it, and make it meaningful.

We would like to sincerely thank Lotsawa Khenpo David Karma Chophel for the translation, and Susan Liu for transcription. Without their devotion and hard work, we would not be able to bring this book to dharma practitioners.

• • • •

TSUM LIBRARY
  January 22, 2023

Supplicating the Gurus

Whenever we recite prayers, meditate, or do puja, it is extremely important that we begin by going for refuge and generating bodhichitta, and that we conclude with dedications. It is taught that it is inappropriate not to do so. Normally we go for refuge to the buddhas, the dharma, and the sangha. In the Secret Mantra Vajrayana, we also go for refuge to the gurus, the yidam deities, and the dharma protectors. In this way, we have six different refuges. We go for refuge to the Buddha as the object or goal of our refuge. The dharma is the path, and the sangha is our companions on the path. The gurus grant us blessings; yidam deities grant us the accomplishments; and dharma protectors dispel obstacles. This is why we go to all six for refuge in the Vajrayana.

When we talk about going for refuge, such as going for refuge to the Buddha, does this mean that the Buddha will reach out his long arms, pluck us out of the lower realms, and liberate us from the samsara? No, it does not work like that. When we practice the dharma, we are saving ourselves from falling into the lower realms. As the Buddha said, you are your own protector and your own refuge. It depends on your own efforts.

Whether we are going for refuge, rousing bodhichitta, reciting prayers, or doing any other practice, we should generate devotion and compassion from deep within. Usually we just recite the words and do the practice only partially. If, instead, we have devotion and faith deep within ourselves, then we will be able to protect ourselves.

In order to develop faith and devotion, we recite prayers such as this one, *Calling the Guru from Afar.* As the note at the beginning of the text says, it should be sung with a beautiful melody because when you sing with a melody, it gives you a strong feeling. That, in turn, helps you develop devotion. If you have a nice voice, then you can sing it nicely. But even if your voice sounds like a dog's or a donkey's, you should still sing it with faith and devotion. By doing so, you will receive the blessings of the gurus.

Calling the Guru from Afar was written by the nineteenth-century master Jamgön Kongtrul Lodrö Thaye. He was instrumental in preserving the teachings of all the lineages of Tibetan Buddhism. He compiled several large collections of practice texts, empowerments, and instructions in what are called the Five Treasuries. In this way, he preserved the empowerments and transmissions of the practices of all Tibetan lineages. He was known as a great master of the Rimé or nonsectarian movement. Reflecting this movement, Calling the Guru from Afar begins with a supplication to our root guru and continues on with supplications to all the gurus of the major Tibetan lineages.

The first two stanzas are prayers to our root gurus as the embodiment of the Three Jewels and Three Roots. The first stanza reads:

> *Lama, think of us. Gracious root lama, think of us.*
> *Essence of the buddhas of the three times,*
> *Source of the true dharma of scripture and realization.*
> *Master of the noble assembly of the sangha,*
> *Who is my root lama, think of us.*

Here we pray to the guru as the embodiment of all Three Jewels. We pray to the guru as the essence of all buddhas of the three times — the past, present, and future — because the guru is the same as the buddhas in teaching the dharma. The Buddha Shakyamuni taught the dharma over two thousand years ago, but we cannot receive the teachings from him directly. We receive them from the guru instead, so he is like the essence of all buddhas. He is also the source from whom we receive the true dharma, and he is the master of the sangha, so in this way we pray to our root guru as the embodiment of the Three Jewels.

In the next stanza, we supplicate the guru as the embodiment of the Three Roots—the root of blessing, the guru; the root of accomplishment, the yidam deities; and the root of activity, the dharma protectors.

> *Great trove of blessing and compassion,*
> *And the accomplishment that all will have,*
> *Buddha activity that grants whatever is desired,*
> *Root lama, think of us.*

When we pray to the guru and rouse our devotion, we are able to receive the blessings of dharma practice, so the guru is the root of all blessings. When we practice the dharma, we develop accomplishments through practices of the yidam deities, but these all come from the guru, so the guru is the embodiment of the yidam deities, the root of accomplishment. We pray to Mahakala and other dharma protectors to perform activity to help us gather what we need to do practice and to dispel obstacles. But the root guru is the one who actually does this for us, so the root guru is the embodiment of the dharma protectors. In this way, we supplicate the root guru as the embodiment of the Three Roots and the Three Jewels.

We also supplicate the guru as the embodiment of the dharmakaya, sambhogakaya, and nirmanakaya. In the next stanza, we pray to the guru as the dharmakaya Amitabha:

> *Lama Amitabha, think of us.*
> *Behold us from the expanse of the dharmakaya, free of fabrication.*
> *We wander in samsara through the force of negative karma;*
> *Bring us to rebirth in your pure land of bliss.*

When we pray to Amitabha, we pray to be reborn in the pure land of Sukhavati so that we can practice the dharma. We also pray to the guru as the sambhogakaya Chenrezik:

> *Lama Chenrezik, think of us.*
> *See us from the expanse of the luminous sambhogakaya.*
> *Pacify completely the suffering of the six realms of beings*
> *And totally transform the three realms of samsara.*

In the Vajrayana, we often recite the six-syllable maṇi mantra, Om ma ṇi Pad Me Hum correct diacritics. The reason why we recite this mantra is that each syllable purifies the suffering of a different realm of samsara—the hells, hungry ghosts, animals, humans, demigods, and gods. Thus we pray to the guru as Chenrezik and recite the maṇi mantra to purify all the beings in the six realms.

We also pray to the guru as an embodiment of Padmasambhava, or Guru Rinpoche:

> *Lama Padmasambhava, think of us.*

Behold us from the luminous lotus of Nga Yab Ling.

In these dark times, swiftly protect with your compassion Tibetan disciples,

And all who are destitute without refuge.

In these dark and degenerate times, when we are experiencing epidemics and wars, there is no better being to pray to than Guru Rinpoche, who has great blessings for protecting beings. Guru Rinpoche is also not separate from our own root guru, so we supplicate our guru as the nirmanakaya Guru Rinpoche.

The next supplication is to Khandro (Skt: Dakini) Yeshe Tsogyal, the consort of Guru Rinpoche:

Lama Yeshe Tsogyal, think of us.
Behold us from the dakinis' city of great bliss.
Bring us, who have committed negative actions,
Across the ocean of samsara to the great city of liberation.

It was Yeshe Tsogyal who collected and compiled all the teachings of Guru Rinpoche, preserving them for future generations. She hid many of Guru Rinpoche's teachings as terma or treasures all over Tibet, where they were later found by great treasure revealers. Included among these teachings are the Könchok Chidu and the Tsechu practices we do at our monastery.

The Eight Great Practice Lineages

When the dharma was brought to Tibet, it was brought over in stages by different lamas and passed down in different lineages. All of these are excellent lineages that can bring disciples to buddhahood, each with slightly different teachings. Among all the different lineages, there came to be eight that are called the Eight Great Practice Lineages. The prayer now continues by praying to the masters of each of these lineages in turn.

1. Nyingma

The first of the eight practice lineages is the Nyingma tradition. There are two stanzas supplicating the Nyingmas:

> *Lamas of the oral transmission and terma lineages, think of us.*
> *Behold us from the expanse of primordial wisdom,*
> *the union of appearance and emptiness.*
> *Break through the dark prison house of our confused mind*
> *And make the sun of realization arise.*
>
> *Omniscient Drime Ozer, think of us.*
> *Behold us from the expanse of the five spontaneous lights.*
> *Help us to perfect the great display of mind, primordially pure,*
> *And to complete the four stages of ati yoga.*

The first of these two stanzas is a general supplication to the masters of the oral transmission of teachings that were passed down from Guru Rinpoche as well as to the masters in the tradition of the terma lineages, the treasures revealed by later great masters. We supplicate them to receive their blessings so that we can receive the teachings on dzogchen and manifest the realization of the dzogchen, which is the nature of our mind.

The second stanza is a supplication to the great master Longchenpa, here called Drime Ozer. He was well known for spreading the teachings of the atiyoga of dzogchen including the pith instructions on alpha purity (emptiness) and spontaneous presence (luminosity.) We pray to him so that we may also develop realization of dzogchen.

• • • •

2. KADAMPA

The second of the Eight Great Practice Lineages is the Kadampa lineage, which we supplicate in the next verse:

Incomparable Atisha and your heart son,
Amidst hundreds of deities, behold us from Tushita.
Bring about the birth in our mind stream of bodhicitta,
The essence of emptiness and compassion.

After the dharma was established in Tibet, it flourished until the reign of King Langdarma, who persecuted Buddhism and nearly wiped it out. He did not entirely succeed. There were some teachings that continued in Tibet, but many practitioners forgot about compassion and bodhichitta. For this reason, Atisha was invited from India to Tibet, where he taught primarily the teachings on lojong or mind training, which help us develop compassion and bodhichitta. Thus we supplicate Atisha to develop loving-kindness, compassion, and bodhichitta.

3. Kagyu

The third of the Eight Great Practice Lineages is the Kagyu. There are three stanzas supplicating the Kagyu, beginning with a supplication to the three forefathers of the Kagyu, Marpa, Milarepa, and Gampopa.

Supreme siddhas, Marpa, Milarepa and Gampopa, think of us.
Behold us from the space of great vajra bliss.
Enable us to attain the supreme siddhi of Mahamudra—
Bliss and emptiness inseparable. Awaken the dharmakaya in our heart.

The reason we pray to these three forefathers is that they brought the instructions on mahamudra from India, mastered them, and passed them down to many students.Because of this, we are actually able to practice these teachings and develop realization. We supplicate in particular to develop realization of mahamudra; to awaken the dharmakaya in our heart and realize that our own mind is the same as a buddha's dharmakaya.

The next stanza is a supplication to the incarnations of the Karmapa:

Lord of the world, Karmapa, think of us.

Behold us from the space where all beings, vast in numbers as the sky, are trained.

Bring us to see that all phenomena are like an illusion, without any true existence,

And to realize appearance and mind arising as the three kayas.

Gampopa's main student was Dusum Khyenpa, the First Karmapa. When he passed away, he came back as the Second Karmapa, Karma Pakshi, and then in successive incarnations to the present Seventeenth Karmapa. They are all the same wisdom mind, so we supplicate all of them to realize the nature of mind.

In the next stanza, we supplicate the masters of all the Kagyu lineages:

Lamas of the four elder and eight younger Kagyu lineages, think of us.
Behold us from the realm of pure appearances that naturally arise.
Clear away the confusion of the four situations,
And bring us to the perfection of experience and realization.

In addition to the Karma Kagyu, there are also several other Kagyu lineages, including the Drikung and Drukpa, for example. All of them have excellent pith instructions on mahamudra that can bring the perfection of the experience of realization. So, we supplicate the masters of these lineages as well.

4. Sakya
The fourth of the great lineages is the Sakya lineage:

Five Sakya forefathers, think of us.
Behold us from the expanse of samsara and nirvana inseparable.
Help us to blend together pure view, meditation and action.
Take us along the supreme path of the secret vajrayana.

In the early Sakya lineage, there were five great masters, three of whom were tantric practitioners and two of whom were monastics. They became known as the Five Sakya Forefathers and taught the instructions of the Path and Its Result.

5. Shangpa

The fifth of the Eight Great Practice Lineages is the Shangpa Kagyu lineage:

Lamas of the unequaled Shangpa Kagyu, think of us.
Behold us from the totally pure realm of Buddhas.
Train us correctly in the methods of practice that bring liberation.
Lead us to discover the path of no more learning, the ultimate union.

The Shangpa Kagyu originated with a yogi named Khyungpo Naljor who went to India and received teachings on the six yogas from Niguma, who had been Naropa's consort. These six yogas became the main practice of the Shangpa Kagyu lineage. The Shangpa lineage also has special instructions on mahamudra that were taught by Tangtong Gyalpo, the master who wrote the Chenrezik practice we often do. The next stanza is a supplication to him:

Great siddha, Thangtong Gyalpo, think of us.
Behold us from the expanse of effortless compassion.
Enable us to attain the discipline that brings realization
Of ultimate non-existence, and to master prana and mind.

Through his practice, Tangtong Gyalpo was able to gain mastery over prana (the winds or qi) and mind. The result of this is that he was able to live to the age of 150. We thus supplicate him to gain such mastery ourselves.

6. Shiche

The sixth great lineage is the Shiche lineage. There are two verses of supplication for this lineage:

Only father, Dampa Sangye, think of us.
Behold us from the space of the accomplishing supreme activity.
Bring into our hearts the blessing of the lineage,
And make auspicious signs arise in all directions.

The Shiche lineage comes from the teaching of Dampa Sangye. The word means pacification—the pacification of all suffering. This lineage emphasizes teachings on interdependence that lead to realization. One of the particular practices of the Shiche tradition is Chöd, which is most closely associated to Machik Lapkyi Drönma:

Only mother, Labkyi Drönma, think of us.
Behold us from the space of prajnaparamita.
Enable us to uproot ego-clinging, the source of pride,
And to see the truth of egolessness, beyond conception.

The practice of Chöd is a way to cut through ego-clinging by imagining giving our body to all the gods and demons. We supplicate Machik Lapkyi Drönma to cut through our ego-clinging and realize the meaning of prajnaparamita.

7. Jonang

The seventh great lineage is the Jonang lineage. There are two stanzas of supplication to the Jonang lineage:

Omniscient Dolpo Sangye, think of us.
Behold us from the space endowed with all supreme aspects.
Help us to bring into the central channel the prana of transference
And to attain the immovable vajra body.

The Jonang lineage was founded by Dolpo Sangye, who spread the view of the Shentong Middle Way. He also was a master of the Kalachakra and the six applications. The special instructions of the Jonang school were upheld and spread further by Jetsun Taranatha, a great scholar and practitioner:

Jetsun Taranatha, think of us.

Behold us from the space of the three mudras.

Help us to travel without obstacle the secret vajra path,

*And bring us to the attainment of a rainbow body, the enjoyment of all
space.*

8. The Approach Practice of the Three Vajras

The last of the Eight Practice Lineages is the Approach Practice of the Three
Vajras. This originated with Orgyenpa, who was a student of the Second
Karmapa Karma Pakshi and teacher of the Third, Rangjung Dorje. This lineage
can be considered part of the Kagyu lineage, so there is no explicit supplication
to it here.

3

Jamyang Khyentse Wangpo and Jamgön Kongtrul

Calling the Guru from Afar next has several verses supplicating two nineteenth-century masters who were instrumental in preserving the teachings of the Eight Great Practice Lineages, Jamyang Khyentse Wangpo and Jamgön Kongtrul Lodrö Thaye. During their lifetimes, some of the teachings of the eight lineages were in danger of being lost. So, these two masters worked together collecting as many teachings of all lineages as they could and compiled them into collections that have been passed down since. They were renowned for their unbiased appreciation of all lineages. First there are three stanzas of supplication to Jamyang Khyentse Wangpo, who is called by a different name in each stanza:

> *Jamyang Khyentse Wangpo, think of us.*
> *Behold us from the space of primordial wisdom*
> *That knows all phenomena in their simplicity and in their vast extent.*
> *Clear away the mental darkness of ignorance.*
> *Increase the luminosity of our supreme intelligence.*
>
> *Osel Tulpay Dorje, think of us.*
> *Behold us from the expanse of the five rainbow lights.*
> *Purify the stains from bindu, prana and mind,*
> *And bring us to the enlightenment of the youthful vase body.*
>
> *Pema Do Ngak Lingpa, think of us.*
> *Behold us from the expanse of unchanging bliss and emptiness*
> *inseparable.*
> *Enable us to fulfill perfectly all the intentions*
> *Of the Buddhas and bodhisattvas.*

Jamyang Khyentse Wangpo studied with many masters, receiving the transmissions of many works from all the different lineages. He compiled a large collection of sadhanas, preserving their lineages for future generations. The next four stanzas are supplications to Jamgön Kongtrul Lodrö Thaye, who is also referred to by different names in each stanza.

Ngakwang Yonten Gyamtso, think of us.
Behold us from the expanse of space and primordial wisdom in union.
May we stop taking appearances to be real.
Develop our ability to carry onto the path whatever arises.

Bodhisattva Lodro Thaye, think of us.
Behold us from your state of loving-kindness and compassion.
Enable us to recognise all beings as our kind parents.
Develop our ability to benefit others from the depths of our hearts.

Pema Gargyi Wangchuk, think of us.
Behold us from the expanse of great bliss and luminosity.
Liberate the five poisons into the five wisdoms.
May our dualistic clinging to loss and gain disappear.

Tenyi Yungdrung Lingpa, think of us.
Behold us from the space where samsara and nirvana are equal.
Engender genuine devotion in our mind.
Bring us to simultaneous realization and liberation.

Like Jamyang Khyentse Wangpo, Jamgön Kongtrul was instrumental in preserving the teachings of all Buddhist teachings. He also helped preserve many teachings of the indigenous Tibetan Bön tradition as well and so, in the last stanza, he is referred to by the name Tenyi Yungdrung. A yungdrung is an important symbol in the Bön tradition.

The last stanza of this passage is a supplication to our own root guru:

Kind root lama, think of us.

Behold us from the place of great bliss on the crown of our head.

Bring us to meet the very face of the dharmakaya, the awareness of our true nature,

And in this very life, bring us to complete enlightenment.

We supplicate the guru so that we can recognize the nature of our own mind as it is and reach complete enlightenment.

Renunciation

Alas, sentient beings like ourselves, who have committed negative actions,
Wander in samsara from beginningless time.
Still experiencing endless suffering,
We do not feel even an instant of repentance.
Lama, think of us. Behold us swiftly with compassion.
Bless us that renunciation arises from the depth of our heart.

The second main section of the text begins with the word "Alas," expressing our sorrow and depression at being in samsara. We and beings like us have accumulated bad karma and committed negative actions from beginningless time. Because of accumulating bad karma without feeling repentance for even an instant, we have wandered in samsara for a very long time. But this is not all. As we wander, we continue to commit unvirtuous acts. As result, we all experience endless suffering.

It is not okay to remain attached to all the "good things" in this world of samsara. Trying to overcome our enemies and please our friends will not help us. It would not be right to continue wasting our life in this way.

We have accumulated the causes for our future rebirths in samsara. That is all done, but from now on, we must avoid having any intentions or thoughts that would lead us to samsara. There is nothing we can do in our great sorrow and depression so we pray to the guru. This is why we say, "Lama, think of us. Behold us swiftly with compassion."

The last line reads, "Bless us that renunciation arises from the depth of our heart." We must have a true wish to achieve the liberation from samsara. To do so, we need to keep pure discipline and practice the roots of virtue.

How should we keep pure discipline? We need to take and keep the vows of individual liberation, bodhisattva vows, and tantric vows. Whenever we take any of these vows, we should have the pure motivation of wishing to achieve liberation from samsara. Without a pure intention, taking the vows is difficult.

This is because, as some masters have said, you will not actually receive the vow unless you have such a motivation.

The Eighth Karmapa Mikyö Dorje wrote that without the intention of liberating ourselves from samsara, we cannot take and receive the vows of individual liberation. In order to develop that, we must turn our minds away from this life. We must have a stable belief in future lives, and even though we are not currently in a lower realm, we must reflect on how the sufferings of the lower realms are unbearable.

Making Our Human Life Meaningful

For this reason, we have no time to waste in this life. Therefore, it is important to be careful and apply both mindfulness and awareness. Our life is being used up in each moment of every day, every month and every year. It is critical for us to devote our body, speech, and mind to the practice of true Dharma. As the next verse reads:

Although we have attained a precious human birth with leisure and resources,

We waste it in vain, constantly distracted by the activities of this hollow life.

When it comes to accomplishing the great goal of liberation,

We are overcome by laziness and return empty-handed from a land filled with jewels.

Lama, think of us. Behold us swiftly with compassion.

Bless us that we make this life meaningful.

If we do not use this life well, it would be pointless. There is a story about this from the life of Milarepa, who lived many years ago. One time, when he was meditating in Nyeshang in Nepal, a hunter named Khyirawa Gönpo Dorje met Milarepa. Milarepa said to him, "It's very difficult to achieve a human birth with eight leisure and ten resources. But this does not mean you. A lifetime like yours has no point, as you spend your lifetime killing sentient beings. You have wasted the eight leisures and ten resources of your precious human body."

We all need to think about our own conduct. Are we making our precious human life meaningful? Every minute, every day, every month, every year, are we using our human life in a way that takes advantage of the eight leisure and ten resources? It's important to examine ourselves carefully.

The second line reads, "We waste it in vain, constantly distracted by the activities of this hollow life." In this lifetime, we have spent a lot of time on pointless activities. We go through a lot of of difficulties and hardship in this lifetime, all for the sake of samsaric pleasures. We have tried our best to gain happiness in various worldly ways, but these all create sufferings in the end.

In order to achieve the pleasures of this lifetime, we cause a lot of harm and violence to animals and other sentient beings. These are ways we try to achieve happiness and pleasure in this lifetime alone. But such actions are an inferior methods of bringing ourselves happiness. They are not unmistaken methods, and do not really bring meaning to this lifetime. By acting in such ways that harm other sentient beings, we are not able to bring ourselves happiness that we desire. For the sake of temporary pleasures, we cause harm to sentient beings without bringing any meaning to our lives at all.

We need to make this lifetime and the next meaningful. We need to use the human body to a good purpose. All of us are dharma practitioners. Some of us have become monks and nuns. Why do people choose to become monks and nuns? It's because they feel revulsion for samsara and they want to do something to make use of their lifetime. In Himalayan regions and Tibet, often parents will see that samsara has no benefit in the final analysis and wish to benefit their children. Though the children do not understand what is going on, their parents send them to a monastery or nunnery. The reason they do this is that they see that, instead of happiness, worldly activities will only bring the sufferings of samsara. So they send their children to monasteries and nunneries in hopes that their children will be liberated from samsara.

When the children are arrive at the monastery, whether they are young monks or nuns, they study reading, writing, and Buddhism at the monastery. Some of them develop a wish for liberation. They make use of the opportunity and fulfill their parents' hope. They are also able to truly serve their root gurus. Those people are able to make a good use of and give meaning to their life.

But some others are unable to do so. They do not have any awareness of samsara. They do not have enough merit from the past. It is as if such people have arrived at an island of jewels, but they let all the jewels slip through their fingers. In the end, they have nothing.

It is similar for us. These days, we are truly extremely fortunate that we have the opportunities to see and hear so many gurus. We can meet and hear

Karmapa, Khenchen Thrangu Rinpoche, and numerous other gurus. But we have to look at ourselves and ask: Are we actually using these opportunities to make our life meaningful?

Even just listening has a benefit. It can give us the wish to practice dharma from the deep within. Are we letting that happen? Mostly we are not. It is as if we have gone somewhere and taken all the jewels in our hands, only to drop them. Although we have the chance to make our life meaningful, we have not. It's really important to develop the wish to devote ourselves solely to practicing dharma.

Death and Impermanence

There is no one on this earth who will not die.
Even now, people are passing away, one after another.
We also soon must die. But, like a fool, we plan to live long.
Lama, think of us. Behold us swiftly with compassion.
Bless us that we curtail all of our scheming.

All of us will die at some point, but most of us still try to make plans, some long-term and some short-term. There are even those who think they will not die. They make no plans, or do not include death in their planning. Science and technology has improved so greatly that we no longer worry about death. It is quite possible that we will get to a point where it might seem that we will never die.

But no matter how many scientific and medical advances there are, it is impossible that some day we will not die. While we wait for the scientific and medical advances, we lose physical and mental energy, strength, and capacity every single day and every year. For example, compare yourself now to how you were a year ago. How have you changed? Your body may have grown a little weaker, and your mind less clear.

Some of us think that we will wait until we retire before we devote ourselves to dharma practice. But if we wait, there is no certainty it will ever happen. As the prayer says, there is no one on earth who will not die. We need to practice now, while we still have the time and the energy. If we are able to practice and gather the accumulations of merit while we are still young, it easier for us to develop realization, it is said, and the dharma practice will be easier and go better.

For example, I am nearly fifty years old, and if I were try to do a hundred thousand prostrations now, it would be very difficult, considering the amount of energy and strength I currently have. But I already did that twice when I was young. All of our bodies and minds are growing weaker and deteriorating as time passes. One day we will all have to go. We must use our body and mind while we can, so it is important for us to realize death and impermanence. As the prayer says, if we plan to live long, we are like fools.

Preparing for Death

We will be separated from our closest friends.

Others will enjoy the wealth we as misers kept.

Even our body we hold so dear will be left behind,

And our consciousness will wander without direction in the bardos of samsara.

Lama, think of us. Behold us swiftly with compassion.

Bless us that we realize the futility of this life.

Every day we lose people whom we love, who are close to us and dear to our hearts. This makes us sad and depressed. In general, the thought of death, and the thought of losing our parents and loved ones, depresses and saddens us. But when we examine this, there are two types of suffering here. First, there is the person who is suffering from dying. They haven't cut their ties to samsara or severed the bonds of affection and such for their family and friends. They do not want to die; they have no desire to leave this body and move on. But they must part from the people they have loved in this lifetime and move on, despite not having any desire to.

We feel very sad when we see people who are close to us pass away. When we see characters in a movie die, we feel sad and sympathize with them. How will we feel when it actually happens to someone who is truly close to us, such as our parents, brothers, sisters, or friends? How will we feel when they pass away?

What can help us in this situation? As I said earlier, we need to cultivate loving-kindness and compassion, meditate on our root guru, and practice the dharma. This will bring us benefits. In the end, we will certainly be parted from everyone and lose everything. Practicing the dharma now will definitely benefit us then. As the prayer says, "Others will enjoy the wealth we as misers kept."

There is a story that illustrates this. Once there was a monk in Tibet who lived to a ripe old age. Many people had given him offerings of butter, cheese, and tsampa, but he just kept all the offerings. He was so miserly that he was unable to use them himself and unwilling to give them away to anyone else. Instead, he hoarded all the goods. He also had two students, but eventually they got into arguments about what to do with everything he had hoarded, and both left him.

Similarly, we also keep things and become stingy with them. This ends up bringing us into conflict with others. Many people, for example, have conflicts with their parents over inheritances, assets, investments, and so forth. Even siblings who had previously got along very well, get into arguments over family heirlooms and perhaps even sue each other. In the end, we will lose everything anyway. Someone else will end up using it. Instead of being so stingy and miserly, we should use our possessions for our dharma practice.

Thus it is important that we should not be miserly. Instead, we should make offerings to the Three Jewels and be generous to those in need. We should use our resources to gather the accumulation of virtue and to practice dharma. We should help and assist people as much as we are able.

One day we will leave this body behind and die. Then we will enter what is called the bardo, the period of time between our death and our next rebirth. Someone might do phowa practice for us, which does work sometimes, though there are differing results. As the Eighth Karmapa Mikyö Dorje said, there are three types of people who do phowa, the best, the middling, and the lowest. When a guru does phowa for the best type of people, they can realize the nature of all phenomena. When the guru does phowa for the middling type, they will be reborn in a pure realm, and when the guru does phowa for the lowest type of people, they will be reborn in a higher realm within samsara.

If we have not practiced the dharma, then at the time of death it will be difficult for us to actually direct our minds and pay attention while phowa is being done. Therefore, it would be difficult for it to be of benefit to us. The reason is that we will feel a great deal of fear and terror at the time of our death. Even if a great master does a phowa for us, our minds will be unable to rest and difficult to direct.

The main point is that when a lama does phowa for us, we are able to direct our minds towards that and be able to be motivated. If we can do that, the phowa will bring us benefits. Otherwise, the phowa is just high words and empty talk.

DEVOTION

From today on, we need to study and practice phowa, then, as it is said, it will be possible for it to beneficial when a lama actually does it for us.

The Bardo

In front, the black darkness of fear waits to take us in.
From behind, we are chased by the fierce red wind of karma.
The hideous messengers of the Lord of Death beat and stab us,
And so we must experience the unbearable sufferings of the lower realms.
Lama, think of us. Behold us swiftly with compassion.
Bless us that we are liberated from the chasms of lower realms.

Once during the time of the Buddha Kashyapa, there was a king who had a wonderful and handsome little boy. But the child died very young. The king, queen, their entourages, and all the courtiers mourned and grieved for a long time. Their minds were filled with sorrow, despair, and suffering.

At that time, an arhat in the kingdom who had clairvoyant powers saw that there was a being stuck in the bardo who could not be released because his parents had spent such a long time grieving. So he went to see the king and told him, "You, the queen, and the people have been mourning for so long that your son is unable to leave the bardo. He has spent three years in the bardo experiencing fear and terror. You should stop grieving. Give up your sorrow and instead make offerings, dress nicely, and make good aspirations. Only if you do this will your son be freed from the sufferings of the bardo." This may also happen to us. We can see that our families or friends are all impermanent. Many of them have already died, and more will die in the future. When that happens, grieving and lamenting too much will bring them no benefit, just as in the story of the king. Instead of mourning, we need to present ourselves well and to make offerings and aspirations. That will be beneficial and will allow the being to be freed from the bardo.

Thus this stanza discusses how grieving for people who has passed away may actually bring them harm. In particular, when a great master passes on to the pure realms, it is said that if the students grieve the loss of their master, it will actually harm the master's future activities.

Looking At Our Own Flaws, Not Others'

We conceal within ourselves a mountain of faults yet put down others
And broadcast their shortcomings though they be minute as a sesame seed.
Though we have not the slightest good qualities,
We boast saying how great we are.
We have the label of dharma practitioners, but practice only non-dharma.
Lama, think of us. Behold us swiftly with compassion.
Bless us that we lose our pride and self-centeredness.

Usually when we see someone, we immediately see their faults. When we look at or think about other people, we only see what is wrong with them. But it is very rare for anyone to actually look for and see their own faults. We hide our own faults so deep inside ourselves that we cannot even see them. We always see other people's faults because we always focus on them. This makes us unable to see our own flaws. Instead, we should do as is taught in the Seven Points of Mind Training: Don't ponder others.

While we spend our time digging up others' faults, we hide our own. Because of this, we are unable to tame our own being and develop positive qualities. We become overly proud, which leads us to act contrary to the dharma. We call ourselves dharma practitioners and have malas, shrines, statues, offerings as well as thangka paintings in our houses. Pictures of lamas hang in our cars. We practice generosity. We say to ourselves that we are dharma practitioners. But, if we really look at ourselves, we actually only spend time on non-dharmic activities. It is meaningless to call ourselves a practitioner.

As a real dharma practitioner, we should take refuge and bodhisattva vows from great masters, or if we are members of the sangha, we take the monastic vows. Even so, we never look at our own faults but look at others' faults instead.

We end up only acting contrary to dharma. This is really terrible. We are like thieves stealing from our own house. We are the thieves, and we are also the victims of the crime.

We are not actually fooling anyone but ourselves. Our dharma practice is just acting on the outside. What we really need to do is to look into the depths of our hearts. Do we actually have the mindfulness, awareness, and carefulness to practice in accordance with Dharma?

10

Uprooting Ego-Clinging

We conceal within the demon of ego-clinging that brings lasting ruin.
All of our thoughts cause the afflictions to increase.
All of our actions have non-virtuous results.
We have not even turned towards the path of liberation.
Lama, think of us. Behold us swiftly with compassion.
Bless us that grasping onto a self be uprooted.

R*uin* means losing everything. It is like when someone has a business that does not go well and nothing works out. In the end, they lose their business and all their capital. They have been ruined. Similarly, we have also been ruined, and why is that? It is because of our strong ego-clinging, which leads us to always experience great loss.

When our ego-clinging is strong, all our intentions and actions only serve to increase our afflictions—greed, hatred, anger, and so forth. As a result, all our actions are unvirtuous. We are unable to act virtuously. We haven't even begun to turn toward the path of liberation and omniscience, much less taken a step in that direction. Instead, we have headed down the wrong path and are stuck in samsara.

This is why the prayer says, "Lama, think of us." The lama means the Karmapa, who is the essence of the Buddhas of three times; our root guru, the Khenchen Thrangu Rinpoche; or Marpa, Milarepa, and Gampopa. We are praying to them to please see us, know us, and grant us blessings to help us to cut through our self-cherishing.

Our habits of self-cherishing are so strong that we no longer control ourselves; we no longer have freedom. We are under the control of that habit of self-cherishing. Although we do need to care for ourselves to some degree, if it crosses a certain threshold, then we lose control over ourselves. As a result, we find ourselves unable to cherish others as we should.

For example, the clothes we wear do not just appear automatically. Instead, it takes the participation of lots of different sentient beings. There are the sheep whose wool is woven, the weavers, the tailors, and so forth. The end product is the clothes we are able to wear which have come about because of other sentient beings. Anything we would like can only happen because of other sentient beings.

But we are unable to think of that. We have such a deep imprints of ego clinging and self-cherishing from the beginningless time that we are unable to awaken the good imprints within ourselves. If we truly want to bring benefit to other sentient beings, we need to say to ourselves every day, "I am going to give up cherishing myself! I am going to turn my mind toward only thinking of other sentient beings." If we can increase the amount we cherish others and nurture that in our minds, we will be able to accomplish all of our aims.

If we can develop loving-kindness and compassion within ourselves, all the dharma we practice will become genuine dharma. We need to look and see what is stronger inside ourselves—the negative afflictions or the positive virtues?

If the positive virtues are weaker, we need to do something to increase and strengthen them. Then our intentions will become virtuous, resulting in virtuous actions. We will not commit unvirtuous actions. Thus we need to change and improve our motivation in order to avoid experiencing the result of birth in the lower realms. If we never change our motivations, we will never experience the good results of virtuous actions.

11

May Our Mind Become Dharma

A little praise makes us happy. A little blame makes us sad.
With a few harsh words we lose the armor of patience.
Even if we see those who are destitute, no compassion arises.
When there is an opportunity to be generous, we are tied in knots by
greed.
Lama, think of us. Behold us swiftly with compassion.
Bless us that our mind be one with the Dharma.

When someone gives us a little bit of praise, we feel happy. When someone points out our faults, we are displeased, annoyed, or angry at them, even if they are family or friends. This causes a lot of difficulties. Generally, in practicing dharma, we should practice patience. But when someone says something we don't like, we get displeased and lose our patience. Though we all have faults, we cannot see them. So people who point out those faults that we cannot see on our own are our loving teachers.

Being happy when praised and unhappy when blamed makes us spend our whole life experiencing difficulties and suffering. It is important not to take pleasure when you are praised and not to worry about when you are criticized. Instead, we should look at our own self and stand on our own two feet, whether we are being praised or criticized. If we can do that, our mind will become stable and happy.

When we are criticized, we need to practice patience. We have someone to practice patience with, and this will bring the results of patience. If there is no one to be patient with, then we can't practice patience at all. Similarly with praise, people might praise us in various different ways. Sometimes people praise in a truly sincerely way, while other times it's just flattery. When it is sincere praise, we should not be happy about it. Instead, we should have an attitude of equanimity. If we do, then everything will go well.

In general, if we hang onto every word other people say, we will end up suffering when others praise or criticize us. But practicing patience will free us of suffering. As it is said in the Seven Points of Mind Training, "Meditate on the kindness of everyone." Everyone does not mean only your family and friends: It also includes your enemies and difficult people. Since other sentient beings give us the opportunity to practice the dharma and patience, we should always practice kindness toward all sentient beings.

We should also remember that when we say harsh and sharp words, we make people feel unhappy, upset, or angry. Just as we want to be happy, other sentient beings want to be happy. For this reason, the Havana Buddha spoke to a king of the nags, those who live in the depth of the oceans, "Saying harsh words to other sentient beings will bring them down to the hells. It is a grave misdeed."

There is a saying: "Don't upset others. Don't lose your way." Upsetting others is a strong misdeed and will end making you unhappy, too. Likewise, maintaining your footing, poise, and patience when others say harsh words to you will bring great benefits. Normally we might seem like a really good person who behaves and practices well, but when some difficult circumstance occurs, we lose our way and have difficulties. We should be able to keep our way at all times, whether we are facing family or outside problems. It's really beneficial to ponder this deep saying repeatedly.

As the prayer then says, when we see people who are poor and have no money or protection, though we see them, we feel no compassion. Actually, we have an opportunity to practice generosity, but we do not act on it. We do not give what we could. Our minds are bound by stinginess and miserliness. When it comes time to go to an expensive restaurant or to buy ourselves clothes or food, we are willing to spend lots of money. But when it is time to be generous to others, we are unable to do so.

We have such strong imprints from our bad karma that we are unable to practice the dharma. This is why we supplicate the guru to think of us and behold us swiftly with compassion. We supplicate the guru to look at us and bless us so that our mind may be one with the dharma. We pray to the guru to bless us so that our mind can be connected to the dharma.

These are powerful, sacred words, if you have strong faith and devotion. If you get goosebumps and feel as if you are on the verge of tears as you pray, reciting this, then it is one hundred percent certain that you will be able to receive the blessings. It is one hundred percent certain that your mind will mix with the dharma.

Gampopa taught in the Jewel Ornament of Liberation that all sentient beings have compassion and buddha nature. It is impossible that any being could lack them. So there is no reason for us to get discouraged or to think that we are unable to develop compassion. All sentient beings have compassion and buddha nature, but it has been hidden by habits from beginningless time and so we do not realize that we have them. Once we know that we do, though, we need to put them to use and practice.

Normally we feel loving-kindness and compassion primarily for those we are close to such as our relatives, friends, and so forth. But is the love and affection we feel for them what we mean when we speak of loving-kindness in the dharma? The loving-kindness taught in the dharma should be one hundred percent generous and unconditional.

But, our love is often very transactional. If we give a bit of love, we expect to receive love in return.

This is a rather mercantile exchange of loving-kindness and compassion. When we consider how it should be in the dharma, we should be able to feel loving-kindness and compassion even when we are unhappy or displeased. That sort of loving-kindness and compassion accords with the dharma and complements our practice. If we have it, we can tame our wild minds and become genuinely able to practice.

Letting Go of Attachment

We think samsara is worthwhile when it is not.
We give up our higher vision for the sake of food and clothes.
Although we have all that is needed, we constantly want more.
Our minds are deceived by unreal, illusory phenomena.
Lama, think of us. Behold us swiftly with compassion.
Bless us that we let go of attachment to this life.

Sometimes, even though we know that samsara is pointless, inside we still expect something from it. We want to bring ourselves happiness and avoid suffering. We may even understand that there is a higher purpose and lasting benefit to virtuous deeds, but still we give it up for the sake of food and clothing.

We have accumulated many misdeeds for the sake of feeding and clothing ourselves. Many people become fishermen or butchers, or work in meat-packing plants and the like. They commit a lot of bad karma all for the sake of food and clothes. For example, consider the people who founded corporations such as KFC and MacDonalds. Their businesses went well and grew year after year, even after their founders had passed away. But how many chickens and cattle have been killed for these restaurants? Who will all those unvirtuous actions and misdeeds ripen upon? It all leads back to the original founder. This is how it is with food and clothing.

It is similar with wealth and power. We need to be content and know when we have enough. If we do not, we will never be satisfied. With power, for example, people start in some small locale and gain some local power. Gradually they move on to larger and larger districts, gaining more and more influence. Eventually they might reach a high governmental position and even become the president or leader of a country. But even then, they are not satisfied with their wealth and power. They've actually come under the control of their insatiable desires.

As the prayer says, we are deceived by unreal, illusory phenomena. They have tricked and deceived us, so we ask our root guru to think of us and bless us to give up on this life entirely. We often talk about needing to view thing as illusory. However, we normally see phenomena as being real. For example, we have all many painful and unpleasant experiences with our bodies. If one tiny bug bites us, we will have an unpleasant feeling of pain. No matter how much pleasure we had been feeling, that experience of pain will override it. We might go outside and recline on the lawn or sit in the shade of a nice tree. But then the mosquitoes come and bite us, so we no longer feel that it is pleasant or nice. One tiny bug can rob us of all our pleasure.

We put a lot of effort into taking care of our bodies, but if we actually look at where most of our suffering originates, it is in the body. No matter how much we pamper it, we always experience pain and suffering. It's like water rushing down a steep mountainside, or a candle whose flame does not stay still but dances back and forth in the wind. We think of our body as a single thing, but that is not how it is. There are millions of organisms inside our body, and to think of it as a single thing is to not understand how it really is.

13

Karmic Cause and Effect

Not able to endure the merest physical or mental pain,
With blind courage, we do not hesitate to fall into lower realms.
Although we see directly the unfailing law of cause and effect,
We do not act virtuously, but increase in our unvirtuous activity.
Lama, think of us. Behold us swiftly with compassion.
Bless us that we come to trust completely in the laws of karma.

We have accumulated many unvirtuous actions with our body, speech, and mind. This causes us suffering that is subtle and unbearable. The misdeeds we have committed will lead us to rebirths in the lower realms. If we are reborn as animals, we will not have any freedom. In the old days, animals could wander freely where they wanted, whether in fields or in forests. They had freedom. But nowadays that is very rare for animals. If we are reborn in the lower realms, we will have no chance to practice the dharma, so we must do everything we can to avoid that happening.

Our misdeeds might also cause us to be reborn in the hells. There are different hells with myriad unbearable agonies, such as the sufferings of extreme heat and cold. If we really understood how much suffering there is in hell, we would faint and lose consciousness out of fear on even just hearing the names of the hells mentioned. We could not stand even the slightest of these tortures.

In past lifetimes, we have been born in the hells many times already. Now we need to recall how much suffering there is there. Karmic cause and effect are unfailing. Even though we may see that, we still do not always act on it. It is critical for us to act virtuously and give up unvirtuous conduct.

The last line is a supplication that we may truly believe in karmic cause and effect. Karmic cause and effect is discussed in many teachings and we have read about it many times. But it is hard to truly incorporate it into our hearts. This is why we pray to the gurus to bless us to develop true belief in it.

Generally, we do not have deep conviction in karmic cause and effect until we understand the sufferings from lower realms. We do not really see it until we fear suffering. A story the Gyalwang Karmapa told at the Kagyu Monlam a few years ago illustrates this. Once, long ago in China, there was a butcher who killed countless pigs every day. Near his slaughterhouse there was a monastery, which would ring its bell every morning. When the butcher heard the bell, he would get up and prepare to butcher hogs.

One night, the abbot of the monastery had a dream in which a child came to him and said, "Abbot, please do not ring the bell tomorrow. If you do, I will be killed." When the abbot woke up, he thought that he could not let that happen, and the next morning he did not ring the bell. It did not wake the butcher, so he did not slaughter any animals, as he normally would have. Later that day, the butcher wondered why they did not ring the bell, so he went to the monastery and asked the abbot. The abbot told him about the dream, and when the butcher heard this, he had a strong feeling and certainty in karmic cause and effect. He recalled how much killing he had done and felt incredible remorse. He gave up killing and gave away all of his knives and equipment for slaughtering. He took an oath to never butcher an animal again and even became vegetarian. This is because he developed a deep conviction in karmic cause and effect. If we develop similar belief, our dharma practice will become dharma itself, and we will be careful of karmic cause and effect.

If the cause is virtuous, the result will be good. If the cause is unvirtuous, the result will be bad. Sometimes the results of karma are visible to us in this lifetime; sometimes they happen in future lifetimes. But often people have a question here because there are people who spend their entire lives acting badly, yet everything works out for them and their lives seem good. And there are other people who,always behave virtuously, but nothing ever works out for them. Their lives are filled with suffering and difficulties.

Why is that? The misdeeds people do in this lifetime do not bring them a good life now. It is the virtues they have done in their past lifetimes that have brought them a good life. When nothing works out for people now, it is because of bad conduct and behavior in past lives: They are experiencing the ripening of past karma in this lifetime. In the Noble Aspiration for Excellent Conduct, we pray that all karma may ripen on us now in this lifetime where we can see it so that we will not need to experience the lower realms in future lifetimes. Even if we are unable to achieve liberation and omniscience in this lifetime, at least we can experience all karmic results visibly in this lifetime.

To give another example of karma, one type of karma is called "visibly experienced." This means you experience the result in the same life as you commit it. According to another story the Gyalwang Karmapa once told, long ago in Tibet there were a teacher and a student. The teacher had very good meditation, high realization, and clairvoyant powers. One day, as he sat in meditation and looked with his clairvoyance, he saw that his student only had seven days left to live. He did not tell his student, but instead said, "Maybe you should go visit your parents and friends for a few days, and then come back."

The student's family lived some distance from the monastery. The student — oblivious to the fact that he only had seven days left — departed from the monastery and came to a river. On the riverbank there were thousands of ants, but waves from the water was lapping away at the bank and carrying many of them away. The student built a little dam around them to prevent the water from washing away, and in this way saved many of their lives. He went home, saw his family, and, as the master had instructed, returned to the monastery on the seventh day. But he did not die.

The teacher wondered why that might have happened, so he once again sat in meditation and looked with his clairvoyant powers. He saw that the student acting to save thousands of lives had prevented his untimely death and instead increased his life span. This is karma that is visibly experienced.

14

Overcoming the Real Enemy— Afflictions

We hate our enemies and cling to friends.
Lost in the darkness of ignorance, we do not know what to accept or reject.
When practicing Dharma, we fall into dullness, drowsiness and sleep.
When not practicing Dharma, we are clever and our senses are clear.
Lama, think of us. Behold us swiftly with compassion.
Bless us to overcome our enemy, afflictions.

There are people in this world whom we think of and call our enemies. The word enemy is potent. We hate our enemies and try to avoid letting them hurt or harm us. We fear they will treat us badly. As we think like this over and over again, our hatred grows stronger and stronger, so that we no longer have any happiness in our mind. We get into arguments or verbal disputes with them. Eventually, if the verbal conflict continues, we might even use our fists or weapons. This all comes from hatred.

Likewise, we are attached and cling to our friends. We think they are different from our enemies and have a bias in favor of our family and friends. But our attachment and clinging prevents us from freeing ourselves from samsara.

All of this happens because of ignorance. In particular, we are ignorant about what we should do and what we should not do. What we should do is act virtuously. What we should not do is act virtuously. We should not hate our enemies and cling to our friends. Being equanimous toward them instead is best.

For example, think how in this lifetime you have treated friends nicely and done all you could for them, only for them to become your enemies in the end. There have been enemies you hated, and continually struggled with, who later became your friends. In this way, we should not harbor hatred towards our enemies and attachment towards our friends. It is as if we are lost in the pitch darkness of ignorance. So, we need to eliminate the darkness of ignorance.

As the text says, when we decide to sit down and meditate, to go to a monastery, to repeat prayers, and the like, our mind begins to cloud over and we fall asleep immediately. But if we talk about something non-dharmic, such as criticizing or scolding others, our minds become incredibly clear.

We see examples in the news, such as what happened in America on January 6, 2021. When things did not work as some people wished, they got angry, brought staves and long poles, destroyed a lot of property, and vandalized the most important building in the country. What they did was harmful and contrary to dharma. It was not even acceptable by worldly standards. This is not the way of upstanding individuals; it is the way of lowlifes. When it comes to doing something non-dharmic, they have a lot of energy and strength. When it comes time to help or protect others, they are not willing to go beyond a certain limit. So here we pray to the guru that we may not be like that ourselves.

As the last line of the verse says, "Bless us to overcome our enemy, the kleshas." The last line of the verse says: Our enemies are the kleshas, the afflictions. In Buddhism, we call the three primary afflictions of greed, hatred and delusion, the three poisons. Our body, speech and mind are like slaves to our afflictions. We need to conquer this enemy and overcome greed, hatred and delusion. We must continually remind ourselves that we must not let the three poisons take control of us. We must do something to stop being under the power of afflictions.

When we realize we are getting angry or feeling hatred, we need to stop it. Otherwise we will get angry at the people around us first, and then at more and more people. Similarly, when we feel dullness or drowsiness when practicing Dharma, we need to block it. Otherwise we will sleep a bit one day, and then sleep more and more day after day. When we feel desire or attachment, we need to stop it. Otherwise we will have more and more attachments for one thing or another, and eventually nothing will work out.

Afflictions are like poisons. We treat the afflictions like friends even though they actually are poisonous. This is why we pray to the lamas to bless us to overcome our enemy, the afflictions.

15

Taming Our Own Mind

From the outside we appear to be genuine Dharma practitioners.

On the inside our minds have not blended with the Dharma.

We conceal our kleshas inside like a poisonous snake.

Yet when difficult situations arise, the hidden faults of a poor practitioner come to light.

Lama, think of us. Behold us swiftly with compassion.

Bless us to be able to tame our mind ourselves.

Whether monastic, tantric practitioners, or laypeople, we look like dharma practitioners on the outside. We seem like peaceful, good people with kind hearts and compassion. But on the inside, our mind has not mixed with the dharma. Like a venomous snake, it appears beautiful on the outside, but if the slightest thing provokes it, it immediately attacks. The afflictions are like poisonous snakes.

The Kadampa masters of the past had a saying: "When the sun shines, you are a practitioner, but when circumstances change, you show that you are not a practitioner." When the sun is shining, it's warm, you've got good food, and everything is lovely, you feel like a great dharma practitioner. You feel love and compassion and think, "If I am not a good practitioner, then who is?" But then the weather turns to be more like Vancouver in winter and rains throughout the season, and on top of that, there is a pandemic and you have to stay at home for months on end. When that happens, you are easily annoyed or upset by the littlest thing. It turns out you are not a real dharma practitioner. We should do our best not be like that.

As it says in the last line of this passage, we must tame our own mind ourselves. If we cannot, who can do it for us? The Gyalwang Karmapa cannot come and tame our mind; nor can Khenchen Thrangu Rinpoche. Even the Havana Buddha cannot come and tame it for us! No one else can help us. We have to tame our mind ourselves.

Sometimes when we get up in the morning, our mind does not feel good. Perhaps we felt a bit off the night before, or perhaps we had a bad dream. In any case, if we give in that bad mood, we will not be able to distinguish what we should do from what we should not, and we will not be able to have a better motivation.

So, if we wake up in that sort of mood, the first step is to recognize it. Then we should think about why our mind does not feel right today. We should examine our mind and meditate for a few minutes on love, kindness and compassion. If we can do that, our mind will become relaxed and peaceful. In this way, we will be able to tame our own mind.

16

Seeing Our Own Faults

Not recognizing our own faults, we take the form of a Dharma practitioner

While engaging in non-dharmic pursuits.

We are habituated to kleshas and unvirtuous activity.

Again and again virtuous intentions arise; again and again they are cut off.

Lama, think of us. Behold us swiftly with compassion.

Bless us that we see our own faults.

Though we look like dharma practitioners, we engage in non-dharmic pursuits. Still we say to ourselves, "I am a practitioner. I have studied and learned a lot, I have good discipline, and I am different from other people." Actually, we are just telling lies about having superior human qualities. Our non-virtues and afflictions naturally increase, and our virtuous intentions naturally cease.

If we are good Dharma practitioners, we have to act like good practitioners. This is why the prayer asks for blessings to see our own faults. If we think about it in terms of society, family, or work, seeing our own faults is very important.

We need to think about what our faults and problems are. By doing this, gradually we will become able to get along with everyone. If we are unable to see our own faults and instead only look for others' faults, then people will feel it, and they will not like us for it. We live in families and society, and we need to get along with other people. If we look only for our own faults and ignore others' faults, we can have a meaningful human life.

17

Taming Our Rigid Mind

With the passing of each day, we come closer and closer to death.
As each day arrives, our mind gets more and more rigid.
Though we serve the lama, our devotion is gradually obscured.
Our love, affection and pure outlook towards our Dharma friends diminishes.
Lama, think of us. Behold us swiftly with compassion.
Bless us to tame our obstinate mind.

As each day passes—yesterday, last week, last month, last year—we grow closer and closer to the end of this life. As we approach death, it is important to tame our own mind and become a better person. If we do not, our mind will become more and more rigid, and even though we serve our gurus, our devotion will gradually be obscured.

Speaking out from experience, when you spend a long time with your root gurus, you stop seeing their qualities and only see their faults instead. Your mind then gets more and more hardened, less and less clear. Like us, our gurus are ordinary individuals. It is important to look for their qualities rather than their faults. Whether we can do this determines whether our devotion and faith will increase or decrease. If you only look for faults, you only see faults. But, the faults you see are not the guru's: They are your own projections you are imposing on the gurus.

It is often said that it is better to see your root guru for a single instant than to have visions of hundreds of yidam deities. The Kagyu lineage has been passed down from Vajradhara through Tilopa, Naropa, and many great lamas. We should have faith and devotion in them. We should go for refuge to them.

We were not born during the time of those lamas, so we do not have the opportunity to see them. But with our root guru, we have the opportunity to actually see them and be with them. For this reason, the root guru is actually better. It is even said that the root guru is better than all the buddhas. Pleasing our root guru is the same as pleasing the yidam deities. It is the same as pleasing all of the buddhas and bodhisattvas in the ten directions. Displeasing our root guru is the same as displeasing all of the buddhas and bodhisattvas in the ten directions. So for that reason, it is important for us to have faith in and devotion for in our root guru.

That is the connection to this prayer, *Calling the Gurus from Afar.* If we see the guru's qualities, it is one hundred percent certain that we will find the blessings that are present in this prayer.

18

Making This Life Meaningful

Although we have attained a precious human birth with leisure and resources, We waste it in vain, constantly distracted by the activities of this hollow life.

When it comes to accomplishing the great goal of liberation,

We are overcome by laziness and return empty-handed from a land filled with jewels.

Lama, think of us. Behold us swiftly with compassion.

Bless us that we make this life meaningful.

When we come to the monastery to participate in a puja, we may be sitting down, doing the puja, with our eyes looking at the text, but our minds wander everywhere else. We do not have enough mindfulness and awareness. We need to be able to let our minds rest continuously, to let our body, speech, and mind just rest and stay still.

The way our body stays still is by sitting up straight. Our speech stays still by reciting the words properly. Our mind stays still by visualizing the yidam deities. In this way, body, speech, and mind are all staying still and resting in the present, and so we are able to receive blessings. If we cannot do that, then our dharma practice is just hollow words.

19

Cherishing Others

All suffering arises from wanting happiness for ourselves.
Enlightenment is attained through benefiting others, it's taught.
We engender bodhichitta, while secretly cherishing our own desires.
We do not benefit others, and further, we even unconsciously harm them.
Lama, think of us. Behold us swiftly with compassion.
Bless us that we are able to exchange self for others.

We all want happiness for ourselves and we cherish ourselves. But in the Buddhist view, there is no self, no soul, no me. This is different from other religions. When we think of "me," we become proud of ourselves. We think, "I am great, I want to be better, I want this and that..." But thinking of "me" creates all our suffering.

When the Buddha first turned the wheel of dharma of the four noble truths in Sarnath, he first said suffering must be known. Though we have been in samsara since beginningless time, our ego-clinging is so strong that we are stuck in the samsara, unable to liberate ourselves. Wherever we are in samsara, there is suffering, but we do not recognize and understand it. We always think, "There's a little suffering but it will finish and I will be happy later." As a result, we cycle through all realms of samsara experience various sufferings. We hope that suffering will run out some day, but it never does. There is no true happiness anywhere in samsara.

We can think about it in terms of this life. The moment a baby is born, they do not laugh or giggle; they cry instead because this is the beginning of samsaric suffering. But we do not understand that. From beginningless time until now, we have been wandering in samsara. Because of strong ego-clinging and self-cherishing, we are unable to benefit others and unable to achieve Buddhahood.

We take refuge vows, and some of us take bodhisattva vows. We request dharma teachings and practice dharmic activities. But in our minds, we harbor covetous thoughts or malicious thoughts towards others. We end up harming people and not being able to achieve enlightenment and liberation.

As many masters have said, the main point of being Buddhist is our conduct. We must do nothing harmful and have the view of interdependence. If we are not able to benefit other people, at the very least we must do nothing that harms anyone. We must practice non-violence and non-harm. This is the most critical aspect of Buddhism.

20

Gratitude

Our lama is actually the appearance of the Buddha himself, but we take him to be an ordinary human being.

We forget the lama's kindness in giving us profound instructions.

We are upset if we do not get what we want.

We see the lama's activity and behaviour through the veil of doubts and wrong views.

Lama, think of us. Behold us swiftly with compassion.

Bless us that free of obscurations, our devotion increase.

Our biggest problem when we practice the dharma is having expectations, hopes, and fears. As Milarepa said:

If you don't capture your own mind inside,
How can capturing others' bodies outside be of any help?
If you want to catch something, it's time to catch your own mind.

Abandon your aggression, and stay right here.
With the outlook that you have right now,
The affliction of aggression is so unbearable.
On the other side of the mountain, you fear you'll lose your prey.
And on this side of the mountain, you hope you will catch it.
With hope and fear, you wander in samsara.

Our root guru, our teachers, the people who sponsor the monastery, and our elders and parents have all been very kind to us. But we only feel grateful to them when we want, and when like what they are saying. Otherwise, we are ungrateful and forget their kindness. And so we ask for their blessings to we will be free of obscurations and our devotion will increase.

21

Recognizing Our Buddha Nature

Our own mind is the Buddha but we do not recognize it.

All thoughts are the dharmakaya, but we do not realize it.

This is the uncontrived natural state, but we cannot sustain it.

This is the true nature of mind, settled into itself, but we are unable to believe it.

Lama, think of us. Behold us swiftly with compassion.

Bless us that self-awareness be liberated on its own.

Death is certain to come, but we are unable to take this to heart.

Genuine Dharma is certain to benefit, but we are unable to practice correctly.

The truth of karma, cause and effect, is certain,

But we do not decide correctly what to give up and accept.

It is certainly necessary to be mindful and alert,

But these qualities are not stable within, and we are carried away by distraction.

Lama, think of us. Behold us swiftly with compassion.

Bless us that we stay mindful with no distractions.

Why do we not recognize the buddha nature that is within ourselves? It is as if there is a big piece of gold inside our house, but it is hidden under the bed or somewhere. We do not even know it is there.Even if we found it, we would not recognize it as gold. But if we do find it and recognize it as gold, then we can use it or sell it. It will be beneficial. Similarly, even though there is buddha nature in our mind, we do not recognize it.

Likewise, the essence of thought is dharmakaya, but we do not recognize it. As a result, we get carried away by our thoughts, while remaining unable to realize the meaning of the thoughts. This is the uncontrived natural state but we can not sustain it. We do not even know what the natural state is.

If we were able to meditate on the nature and rest without contriving or altering our mind, we could see emptiness. But even if we are able to see that, we are unable to sustain it for an extended period of time and end up instead in a contrived state of mind. We are unable to have confidence in the true nature of mind settled in itself because of our afflictions and impure karma. So we say, "Lama, think of us! Behold us swiftly with compassion. Help us to recognize and understand the natural state itself is the nature of mind. Bless us that we are able to sustain the uncontrived natural state. Bless us to recognize our mind is Buddha and our thoughts are Dharmakaya."

It is extremely important to meditate regularly. Consider the innumerable buddhas in all realms: They all achieved buddhahood by meditating. We will not be able to reach buddhahood by just studying or listening. We have to go through all three steps of listening, contemplating, and meditating. That is how to reach buddhahood.

So, we should meditate regularly. For example, you can do a half or an hour of shamatha meditation in the morning, focusing either on your own breath or on a support. With your body sitting up straight, the channels inside your body are straight and then the mind will run straight. Let your mind rest as it will be. By doing this, you will naturally feel happiness and pleasure in this lifetime. It will also be beneficial for this and future lifetimes. You will be doing something that will make your human life meaningful.

Nowadays we normally spend all day with phones in our hand checking social media. What if we were always checking our mind instead? It is important to take care of our mind. So we should practice frequently. This will bring us mental happiness and also increase our loving-kindness and compassion.

Usually we take good care of external things, such as our appearance, health and so forth, but this does not help our mind at all. Of course, if it's cold, we need to wear warm clothes. Other than that, worrying won't help. Practicing shamatha and insight meditation will take care of our mind.

Sometimes, if we cling to ourselves strongly, we are not able to do the meditation. In this situation, we can meditate on ourselves as any of the various yidam deities, for example visualizing yourself as Medicine Buddha, Tara, or any other deity, in order to keep our mindfulness. This will definitely help us.

I would like to share some of my own experiences. You've all known me for many years. It's quite possible that you think to yourself that lama gets a sweet life staying at the nice monastery. But it's actually quite opposite. Many years ago I met a lama in Nepal who once said that maintaining a monastery is a lot more difficult than building a monastery. At that time, I said to myself, "How could that be?" Now, I have come here, built the monastery, started a small sangha, and had students and sponsors. I have to keep connections with everyone. You might think that I stay at the monastery and have left samsara. That would be really nice, but left samsara? Sometimes I feel there are more problems and more samsara in the monastery.

So how do I deal with this? When I get up early in the morning, I do some meditation. No matter what situations occur in the day, the meditation helps me to be able to handle them. Some days when I am really busy and do not have time to meditate, it's harder to deal with the situations. It's like the words saying from the prayer: From outside you look like a Dharma practitioner, but from inside you are hiding all your faults. When circumstances arise, you will lose it. So my morning practice really helps me.

I am an ordinary monk, nearly fifty years old, who does not have any realization. Because it is not easy to practice and at the same time to maintain a monastery, sometimes I ask myself whether would it just be better to leave and go off into the mountains or to some isolated places for retreat and meditation. What keeps me here is that I always remember the great kindness of our root guru, Khenchen Thrangu Rinpoche. He is close to 90 and has done so many great things in his lifetime. If I were to make some sort of a scene and go off for retreat, what would my root guru think about that? I think if I displease my root guru, it will be the same as displeasing all the buddhas and bodhisattvas in the ten directions.

So, I do as my root guru has taught. I am an ordinary person without any particular qualities or realization, but because of the blessings from Rinpoche,

I have come here, and I do what I can. This gives meaning to my life. Doing meditation every day helps me in my situation. I think if you do the same every morning, it will help, no matter what happens during the day.

22

Friends in a Degenerate Age

Out of previous negative karma, we are born at the end of this degenerate time.

All our previous actions have become the cause of suffering.

Bad friends cast over us the shadow of their negative actions.

Our practice of virtue is corrupted by meaningless gossip.

Lama, think of us. Behold us swiftly with compassion.

Bless us that we take the Dharma deep to heart.

As the great, compassionate Guru Rinpoche said, we are living in a degenerate age. There are more and more things to think about and we have become smarter as well as more clever. This has brought improvements in terms of the external things of this life. But, internally, our mental suffering has increased. We feel more trepidation and fear. Everything we have done up to this point has become the cause of all our current suffering.

If we have bad friends, the shadow of their misdeeds falls on us, and our practice of virtue is corrupted by meaningless gossip. Having bad friends who act negatively may affect us. If our friends are good friends who speak about Dharma and are careful in their actions because of karmic cause and effect, that will influence our own characters and actions positively. But if our friends have bad attitudes, harbor malice toward others, do not think about karmic cause and effect, or criticize the gurus, their shadow will fall upon us. We may eventually become like them.

It is like a sandalwood tree in middle of a forest—the beautiful scent of the sandalwood tree will eventually be absorbed by all the trees around it and they will also smell good. In the same way, if we are around by good friends, we will become good people. Otherwise, we will be carried away by meaningless conversations and neglect our practice. It is extremely important to give up bad friends.

Practicing Dharma Properly

At first there is nothing but dharma on our mind,
But at the end, the result is the cause of samsara and the lower realms.
The harvest of liberation is destroyed by the frost of unvirtuous activity.
We, like wild savages, have lost our ultimate vision.
Lama, think of us. Behold us swiftly with compassion.
Bless us that within we bring the genuine dharma to perfection.

At the beginning, we think only about dharma and want only to practice dharma. Though we try to practice it well, we end up not doing it properly. Dharma practice becomes a custom and ritual. We use dharma to do business, politics, or other non-dharmic things. We end up committing the ten non-virtues and the five heinous actions. As a result, we will be reborn in the lower realms.

It is as if the harvest of liberation is destroyed by the frost of unvirtuous activity. In spring, we plant the seeds and grow into crop. But when a hailstorm comes, it will destroy the entire crop. In the same way, when we try to practice dharma, the hailstorm of our unvirtuous actions will destroy our efforts. Though we look like dharma practitioners, we are like wild savages and have lost our ultimate vision. Everything we do becomes a cause of samsara and birth in the lower realms. Lama, please behold us swiftly with compassion so that this may not happen to us.

Requesting Blessings

Bless us that repentance arise deep from within.
Bless us that we curtail all our scheming.
Bless us that from the depth of our heart we remember death.
Bless us that we develop certainty in the laws of karma.
Bless us that our path is free from obstacles.
Bless us that we are able to exert ourselves in practice.
Bless us that we bring difficult situations onto the path.
Bless us that antidotes, through their own power, are completely effective.
Bless us that genuine devotion arise.
Bless us that we see the very face of the mind's true nature.
Bless us that self-awareness awaken in the centre of our heart.
Bless us that confused appearances are completely eliminated.
Bless us that we achieve enlightenment in one lifetime.

This passage is easy to understand; I don't think you will have any problem understanding it.

Longing for the Guru

We pray to you, precious lama.
Kind lama, lord of Dharma, we call out to you with longing.
For us, unworthy ones, you are the only hope.
Bless us that your mind blends with ours.

Now we will recite the next four lines of the supplication. Please imagine your root guru in front of yourself and sing along with me. The melody is beautiful. As I said in the beginning, if you have a nice voice, then sing it with a nice voice and if your voice is like a dog's, then sing it with a dog's voice. It really doesn't matter. If your dog voice helps you generate faith and devotion in your root guru, that is great.

The main point is that you should think as is said in a famous verse, "The guru is the yidam; the guru is the dakini. The guru is the dharma protector; there's no one else but you." As it says here, we are calling the guru. Calling is something we do when we are far away. If the guru were nearby, we would not need to call. Wherever the guru is, whether Europe, Nepal, India, or Tibet, we call them with fervent longing, joining our hears with the prayer.

The third line says, "For us unworthy ones, you are the only hope." You are the only one who can help in this lifetime. We do not have anyone else but you to ask. . We have to place all our hopes in the guru.

The last line reads, "Bless us that your mind blends with ours." As you read this line, imagine the guru's body, speech, and mind as a white oṃ in the guru's forehead, a red āḥ in the guru's throat, and a blue hūṃ in the guru's heart. They shine light rays that dissolve into you through your own forehead, throat, and heart. Not only do they dissolve into you, but you then become inseparable from your root guru. The guru is vividly present in front of you, and you are calling the guru from afar. Whether we are reciting this prayer, doing the four preliminary practices, or reciting the four mothers prayer in the guru yoga, we imagine taking the four empowerments in this way. Doing this is very beneficial.

We then close the practice with dedicating the merit for the benefit of all beings:

By this merit, may I attain omniscience,
Defeat the enemy wrongdoing, and free
All wanderers from the ocean of existence
Churned by great waves of birth, age, sickness, and death.

About the Author

Dungse Lama Pema Rinpoche was born into a family of great Buddhist practitioners, whose ancestry goes back to the 13th century Buddhist master Guru Chokyi Wangchuk. Lama Pema first learned Buddhist practice and teachings from his father at a very young age.

In 1981, he left his family monastery in remote Tsum valley, Nepal, and became Buddhist Monk in Thrangu Monastery while still a young boy. Since then Lama Pema has studied extensively on philosophies, rituals and meditation techniques from various Buddhist teachers, particularly from his Guru, The Very Venerable Ninth Khenchen Thrangu Rinpoche.

In 1989, Lama Pema received full ordination of a Bhikshu from Khenchen Thrangu Rinpoche.

In 1997, he completed his three year retreat at Namo Buddha in Nepal under the guidance of Khenchen Thrangu Rinpoche. He held many important positions serving his Guru, from school Principal at Shree Mangal Dvip Boarding school to Vajra Master at Thrangu Monastery. In 2003, Lama Pema travelled to Vancouver, Canada to establish Thrangu Monastery Canada, and is the resident Abbot there.

Dungse Lama Pema has dedicated his life to practicing and teaching the Dharma, and travels extensively worldwide.

Read more at https://thrangumonastery.org.